Praise for Show UP Be BOLD Play BIG

If you want easy to implement, practical strategies for making your life better and your business stronger then you're holding it in your hands. Kim's 'kitchen table' wisdom will put you on the path to more success and happiness, without having to make radical changes in your life. This book just makes sense!

Marti Barletta, Author of *Marketing to Women: How to Increase Your Share of the World's Largest Market* and *Prime Time Women: How to Win the Hearts, Minds, and Business of Boomer Big Spenders*

Kim Hodous gives so many great easy to follow, yet powerful strategies for success in her beautiful book, *Show Up, Be Bold, Play Big*. This valuable book will help you create more success, ease and fun in your life! I highly recommend it.

Dr. Eve Agee, Best-Selling Author of *The Uterine Health Companion: A Holistic Guide to Lifelong Wellness*

Kim systematically outlines 33 simple strategies that truly can transform your success and happiness. It's like a User's Guide for living a bigger life and having a better business.

Jill Lublin, International Speaker and Author of 3 Best-Selling books including, *Get Noticed...Get Referrals: Build Your Client Base and Your Business by Making a Name For Yourself*

You can flip this book open to any page and find something meaningful that you can use right away. This isn't 'theory' – it's full of practical tips and tools you can put to use in your life immediately. Great information! Thanks, Kim.

Deborah Kagan, Sensual Lifestyle Specialist & Best-Selling Author of *Find Your ME Spot*

Kim's strategies just make sense. Although they're small things, they make a big impact. When you're ready to show up, be bold, and play big – Kim will show you how! Don't miss this gem of a resource for making big changes in simple ways.

Meryl Hershey Beck, M.A., M.Ed., LPCC, Best Selling Author of *STOP EATING YOUR HEART OUT: The 21-Day Program to Free Yourself from Emotional Eating*

If what you are looking for is SUCCESS without compromising your lifestlye, Kim Hodous' book, *Show Up, Be Bold, Play Big*, is for you. Kim's approach is simple yet thorough – from her proven strategies for creating success that's enduring to her methodologies that instill happiness that is genuine and lasting. If this is the type of success you're looking for, look no further. Get inside this book NOW, and be ready to achieve your desires as you learn to Show Up, Be Bold and Play Big!

Kym Belden, Fitness & Sports Trainer & Body Performance Coach, and Author of *Freeing Your Body, Releasing Your Mind, Moving You into Action and coauthor of Power to Change*

Offering pithy and practical advice clearly born of life experience, Kim Hodous has created a concise playlist for outrageous success both in business and in life. Filled with thoughtful interactive exercises, Kim clearly delivers on her promise to help you show up, be bold and play bigger than you've ever imagined possible.

Jeanette DePatie (AKA The Fat Chick) Top-Selling Author of *The Fat Chick*

As a Lifestyle Remodeling Specialist and Professional Organizer, I found Kim's thirty-three tips to be right on the mark for those who are ready to take their life to the next level. No matter what situation you are facing when you pick up this book, you will find strategies that can be immediately applied with benefits following soon after. Kim is an extraordinary person with simple yet profound insights that she shares in this book; it's one you can keep close at hand and read over and over again.

Virginia Barkley, Author of *Clutter Busting for Busy Women*

Show Up, Be Bold, Play Big, is a home run! Kim Hodous, through her personal story, shows us how to have it all! I have coached start ups to Fortune 500 companies and yet within one hour of reading Kim's book I was able to share one of her business success tools that will produce thousands of dollars in additional income to a client! This is not just a touching story, but a direct roadmap that anyone can follow to predictably receive success in business and life.

Gary Barnes, The Traction Coach, Gary Barnes International and author of *Into the Night*

If you want to show up, be bold, and play big in your business, you must read Kim Hodous' book. It is simple but genius. Thanks, Kim for helping me be bold in my business.

Sasha Spinner, Author of *Sasha's Rules for Starting Your Own Successful Business in Under 90 Days*. www.sashasrules.com

Show Up, Be Bold, Play Big is one of the most inspirational, educational, and moving reads I've come across. Kim Hodous has lived a journey riddled with the kinds of massive obstacles few have to endure...and she has TRIUMPHED! Here, she offers deep wisdom and practical insights in an incredibly thoughtful, engaging, useful and entertaining way.

Callan Rush, CEO Leader to Luminary Training

Kim definitely lives the philosophy of showing up, being bold and playing big. I'm grateful she's finally compiled the strategies that got her there. You're sure to learn how to live a bigger life and find more success through the information she shares.

Michelle Prince, Best-Selling Author of *Winning In Life Now*

Kim's book is full of insight and wisdom. I like how she's taken her life experiences and pinpointed the strategies she used to build a successful company and create true happiness. Her step-by-step process is easy for me to understand and apply to my own life - immediately. I'm excited to get started.

Barbara Khozam, Author of *How Organizations Deliver BAD Customer Service (and Strategies that Turn in Around!)* www.badcustomerservicetips.com

If you want more success and happiness in your life, this book is a must read! Kim provides practical strategies that anyone can easily apply to get you playing at a higher level.

Julianne Gardner, Founder of www.ButterflyEffectMovement.com, Author of *Butterfly Effect Movement: Discover Your True Self, Change Your Circumstances & Live Your Life Purpose*

If you have ever wondered how you can create wealth and success with only an idea and a kitchen table, then follow Kim's simple strategies for yourself. If you were only existing in your life, these strategies will definitely reveal the secrets to Show Up, Be Bold and Play Big! Then you'll be living your dreams, not just imagining them!

Andrea Adams-Miller, MS, CHES, CEO and Founder, IgniteYourRelationships.com

Show UP Be BOLD
Play BIG

33 Strategies for Outrageous Success and Lasting Happiness

from a Former Stay-at-Home Mom Who Built a

7- Figure Business From Her Kitchen Table

THE KITCHEN TABLE CEO™

KIMHODOUS

This book is dedicated to my amazing family and all those courageous souls who show up, be bold and play big each day in their own lives.

Contents

Preface

My core philosophy for living is this:
show up, be bold, play big.

It's not a complex formula. It's actually pretty simple, isn't it? The wonderful thing is that it works for all areas of life. I want life to be easy and for everything to be bundled up into one juicy adventure. I don't want compartments like "work life," "family life," "play time," "church time," and "me time." I've always believed that life should be integrated. I want for each day to hold wonder and excitement, and for every area of my life to be fun and rewarding. I've found it can be when we start to show up, be bold and play big.

Showing up, being bold and playing big is how I've lived most of my life. According to my mom, I came out of the womb with this philosophy already genetically encoded. I showed up on my own terms and when I was ready. I was two weeks overdue, but when I decided to come out, I wasted no time. I was born in the hallway of the hospital on a gurney before they could even get my mom into a room!

At the age of four I was picking grapes out of the fruit cocktail at pre-school because I heard the migrant workers were being mistreated, and at the ripe old age of six I planned my own birthday party because I thought my parents weren't going to have one for me.

I have always been fully engaged in life, pushing the envelope on every level and believing I could do something that would make a difference.

The Shift

My life right now is pretty sweet. I have a large, loving family; a marriage that spans over twenty-five years; and a company that requires less than ten hours a week of my time but pays me like a full-time CEO. I use my passion for teaching to coach individuals to greater success and lasting happiness, and I speak professionally on the same topic. Every week I get to work out with a personal trainer, study and practice martial arts with a seventh-degree black belt and teach yoga. I have a rich spiritual life. I meditate daily and spend a week alone in silence every year on the lake. I have close friendships, and am surrounded by people who love and support me.

But it wasn't always this way.

I might have come out of the womb wired for sound, but somewhere along the way I lost my mojo. Maybe you've experienced it in your own life. You come out of college so excited about life and ready to make your impact in the world, and then things happen. Disappointments.

Preface

Frustrations. Heartbreak. And all of a sudden you're not showing up, you don't have the *chutzpah* to be bold, and as far as playing big, you're not even sure you want to play!

In the fall of 1993, that was where I found myself.

Between 1987 and 1992 my husband Robert and I were blessed with four beautiful children. By Thanksgiving of 1993 we had a five-year-old, a three-year-old, a one-and-a-half-year-old, and a six-month-old. I loved being a mother, but four children in five years was a lot of work! I was exhausted, fifty pounds overweight, and just trying to make it through each day. I was in what I call "dog paddle mode." I was just doing what I had to every day to keep my head above water.

On the Wednesday before Thanksgiving, my daughter Chelsea, who was only eighteen-months-old, was finishing her third round of antibiotics to clear an ear infection — but she wasn't improving. So I called our family physician to get Chelsea an appointment before the Thanksgiving holiday the following day.

That's when our world started to unravel.

The physician decided to run some blood work to see what was going on. He worked out of the same medical building as my husband, who was a dentist. When the doctor came to me and said, "You need to go get your husband right now," I knew this wasn't good. If you're a parent, you probably know what I'm talking about. It's a phone call, a question asked in a certain way, an unexpected knock on the door, and you know your life is about to change.

The doctor informed us that Chelsea's blood looked leukemic. He couldn't officially confirm the diagnosis, but we had an appointment with a pediatric oncologist at the Children's Cancer Center the next morning at seven. The next day was Thanksgiving, but that didn't matter. He told us to get the other children taken care of, pack our bags immediately and get to Phoenix for our appointment.

The next six months would lead us down a path I never planned on traveling. Chelsea was diagnosed with leukemia. At that time childhood leukemia had about a 70% cure rate. But she didn't have childhood leukemia. She had the very worst kind of adult leukemia. We learned about platelets and white blood cell counts and hemoglobin levels. Chelsea would endure whole body systemic radiation and massive doses of chemotherapy, and even a bone marrow transplant from her younger brother on his first birthday.

It was to no avail. On the night of May 21st, six months after diagnosis, my husband and I sat on the ninth floor of the Minneapolis Pediatric Bone Marrow unit, with Chelsea cradled between us, as she took her last breath. I remember looking up after Chelsea took that last breath and saying, "God, breathe life into her. Bring her back." But that wasn't her path. Chelsea was gone.

We held her, we held each other, and then we went to the Ronald McDonald House and got her three siblings so they could say their good-byes to their little sister. At the hospital, we had one more moment as a complete family, and then we walked away from that room, our lives irrevocably changed.

Nothing Will Ever Be the Same

The morning after Chelsea died, we all went back to the Ronald McDonald House that had been our home for three months. My mom had taken the kids outside to play and Robert and I had a quiet moment together. I remember it so well. We were on the couch just being with each other, and he said, "You know, life's never going to be the same." In agreement I said, "You're right, life's never going to be the same." And then, in that moment, I realized if life was never going to be the same, it could only do one of two things: life could get better or life could get worse.

And so I pledged in that moment to make life better. To make my life better, to make my kids' lives better, and to make the lives of every person I met better if it was in my power to do so. I had no other choice. Life could only get better or it could get worse, because it surely wasn't going to stay the same.

Following Chelsea's death, I went home and I healed. I healed not only my heart, but I healed my life. I always say it was through Chelsea's dying that I learned to fully live. Chelsea was the wake-up call for me to stop merely existing and to get back to showing up, being bold and playing big. That's what she did in her short life. She showed up, shook it up and took it over the top. I remember someone saying to me, "It's such a shame her life was cut short." I immediately responded that it was not. She lived every day she was meant to live, and she lived it to the fullest. I was determined to get back to that place in my own life.

The next few years were a journey of healing and forgiving, of loving and letting go, of learning and living. It was one of the most painful times and one of the most poignant times of my life. I grew in ways I never imagined during those years. I gained an awareness about life that I never had before. I found beauty and sacredness in things that had previously seemed small and insignificant. I complained less. I laughed every day. I cried every day. I appreciated more. I got healthy. I hugged more. I was grateful for everything. I was awed by life again. I was rediscovering myself and the art of living fully. I was beginning to once again show up, be bold and play big.

It wasn't an easy road. It took something as painful as the death of my daughter for me to fight hard enough to get my zest for life back. But when I was back, I was back 100%!

And when I was back 100%, I realized I *wanted* to go back to work. I recognized that work fills up a part of me that being a parent doesn't. It's not that I value my family or my role as parent less than my career;

I just need both things in my life to bring me to the biggest me I can be. That was one of the greatest lessons Chelsea's death taught me — that we've all got one shot at life. There's no rewind button. There's no do-over. No second chance. So we better get busy living and doing what fills us up and what we were put here to do!

As I began to contemplate what I wanted to do for work, I realized that my work had to come from a different place than before. This is when I realized that I didn't want "work" and "family" and "me time" as separate categories; they all had to integrate together.

I wanted my kids to be able to come through my office after school, and although I'm not a counselor or a minister, I wanted my company to be where I live out my spirituality by the way I run my business, interact with my team, and treat my clients. I wanted to have fun at work and I don't mind if play is strenuous — like a 9-hour hike or a 30 mile bike ride!

Going to college and becoming a school teacher was what my parents wanted for me. But when I looked into the depths of my soul and made a choice, a choice based on what I wanted in life, I realized I wanted something different.

Showing Up, Being Bold, and Playing Big

Despite the deep grief I'd experienced, I was back to living my life from my core philosophy. I was showing up and being bold and playing big. It had nothing to do with following the rules, fitting in the box or traveling the traditional path. I didn't know what I wanted to do. I just knew what I *didn't* want to do. So I tried all kinds of things — waitressing, corporate communications, belly dancing, network marketing, personal training, sales, and I know there were others I've put out of my mind.

But it was Rockwood Jewelry that grew organically from living the philosophy of showing up, being bold, and playing big. It turned out that this simple philosophy, which allowed me to craft a full life, also helped me build a successful business.

Trust me, I'm no genius. I've failed as much as I've succeeded. I have neither formal training nor a degree in business. I've never taken a marketing or an accounting course. My only training is as a high school History or English teacher. My family doesn't have a history of success in the free enterprise system. My dad's a minister and my mom's a retired school teacher. Neither of them has ever owned or even attempted to start their own business. (I do remember my mom doing some sewing in the summers to make extra cash, but I'm not sure that counts.) There were never discussions around our family table about profit margins, advertising budgets, or cash flow. My dad was a peace activist, so we would hotly debate the death penalty, civil rights and the Fourteenth Amendment. I know that helped mold me into who I am, but it didn't give me any understanding of or insight into the world of business.

Preface

My only real credential for writing a book on business is that I started one at my kitchen table. And it flourished. For the past ten years, I've been CEO of Rockwood Jewelry Company. We specialize in providing quality jewelry for fundraising events and campaigns. I've tried to run this company using my head. I've learned the best way is by following my gut and listening to my heart.

My theory is that there are a lot of little things we can do in business, and in life, that can make a *big* difference. The chapters in this book are a compilation of all those little things that made a big difference for me — and they can for you, too! They're really quite simple and you can apply them instantly. In fact, there are *no* radical changes you need to make in your everyday life. There are just simple little strategies to implement and I've provided practical exercises to get you started. Some of them you are probably already doing. Some may not fit for you, but who knows — just one could push you to the next level or give you the major ah-ha you were missing!

The Kitchen Table CEO™

I didn't become the Kitchen Table CEO by accident. To me, the kitchen table represents the heart of the family. And that's at the heart of this book. It's about combining business and family and creating a business and, most importantly, a lifestyle that works for you.

For me, it isn't about hitting a certain sales number each year. More than once, what I've wanted out of my business has shifted, morphed, made 180-degree radical turns, and then come back to center. What works one year may not work the next. I'm all about looking at business as a vehicle to provide for us what we choose at any given time in our lives. Implementing certain strategies so that our businesses are stable and our success predictable; implementing certain practices in our lives so our happiness is genuine and lasting. These are the strategies I am going to share in this book.

Some of the best advice my mom ever gave me — often while chatting at her kitchen table — was to love every day of my life. I believe it's possible. To take the good with the bad and toss 'em all up together so that in the end, we live a life we love. I want your business not to become the focus of your life, but to become an extension of the way you're living. All parts of your world working together to support you, however you choose for it to look.

In the chapters that follow I'm going to ask you to do some simple exercises to integrate the concepts taught in each strategy. They won't take long but the results may surprise you. If you're like me and you'd prefer to do these on a separate piece of paper, go to www. kimhodous.com/bookexercises.pdf and download all the exercises in booklet format. Ready? OK!

Show Up. Be Bold. Play Big. *Let's go!*

Big Love,

Kim

Show Up. Be Bold. Play Big.

Part One: Show Up

To show up is to be consciously awake in each moment — and then to make decisions from that place of total awareness. Showing up is about what you *do* to create real-world success in your business and in your life. To be present in your life means to see the wonder in every moment. To be awake to possibilities. To see things most people miss when just going through the motions. When you wake up and are fully present, magic will start to happen in your life, in your business, and in your world.

1

Wake Up and Pay Attention

*If I have ever made any valuable discoveries, it has been owing more to **patient attention** than to any other talent.*

Sir Isaac Newton

Waking up is about being aware of, and paying attention to, what is taking place around us. Then, once we're awake and aware, we need to put our focus on those things that matter.

I was a stay-at-home mom enjoying my hobby of making jewelry at the kitchen table with my teenage daughters, when a friend asked to buy one of our bracelets to give as a gift. I could have simply obliged, pocketed the fifteen dollars, and continued with my hobby. But I was paying attention, so I decided to test the waters with a home-made website. I sold a few bracelets each month on the website, and it was from two of these early sales that my first large order (2,000 bracelets) and the direction of my company (fundraising) were born.

When we're paying attention, it's critical that we pay attention *to what matters*. In some companies the office talk is about who came back five minutes late from lunch, parked in the wrong spot, or whose skirt is too short. If you want to show up in a bigger way, you must place your focus on what matters, at all times. Are you focused on what kind of car your neighbor is driving and who just lost their job, or are you focused on building lasting relationships and a deeper connection with the people who inhabit your world?

I believe our culture is facing a crisis of focus. Instead of paying attention to the important things, we're often focused on the unimportant and trivial. Look at our news; unless it's sensational and disturbing, it's not going to make the front page. In our lives and our businesses, we really need to pay attention to what matters. In business, that's our people (customers, clients, and co-workers) and our 'operation' (products, processes, and prosperity). In our personal lives, we need to focus on our people (family, friends, neighbors, community) and we need to pay attention to the temple that is our body (health, spiritual growth, play and creativity.)

Exercise: Paying Attention

Think back over this past week and recall an instance where something came up that got your attention. It might be something small or relatively insignificant, but it's stayed in the back of your mind. At work it might be the way an employee responded to a client question or the way a box looked before shipping. In life it might be the way your pants felt a bit tight or how you unexpectedly snapped at one of your children before bedtime. If you weren't happy with the way the box looked before shipping, maybe you're also not happy with the way the entrance to your office looks and the first impression you're making to clients. It's significant because this small thing you noticed is really indicative of something much larger. Perhaps you snapped at one of your children because there's really an issue with your spouse you need to clear up that has you unsettled. Find the hidden gem of realization behind that seemingly small detail you noticed when you were paying attention.

If you can't think of something right now, keep paying attention. Something will come up this week.

BUSINESS INSTANCE:

REALIZATION:

LIFE INSTANCE:

REALIZATION:

Think Long, Think Wrong

*If you want to be successful,
you must stop making excuses and instead
make decisions promptly and definitely.*

Napoleon Hill, American author

Many of us were taught as young children to think before we act. That might be good advice for an impetuous child. But I've found that in business, taking quick and decisive action is often the key to change and growth.

At a recent trade show where I book about 70% of my business, a client asked if we had paw print earrings. We didn't but we had a paw print necklace. When I saw the client was about to leave my booth, I said, "But here's our necklace and we could get this made into earrings for you." The client had been to every other jewelry vendor, and although a few had earrings with paw prints on them, she felt ours were the perfect size and she was interested in moving forward with the design. I had to work out the details once we got home — pricing, packaging, product specs — but I got the sale. If I had thought too long about it, I would have missed the opportunity.

In life, we also have the opportunity to live more effectively if we react quickly. Last winter, I was exiting Sam's Club and there was a young lady at the door checking receipts. It was a blistering cold day and she had no mittens. She kept blowing on her fingers and I could tell she was miserable. As I approached she said, "I forgot my mittens and I've got seven more hours here."

Without thinking, I whipped off my mittens and said, "Here, take mine. I'll be heading home soon." Her eyes welled up with tears and I could feel her deep gratitude for this simple act. They were a 99-cent pair of mittens for goodness sakes! However, if I had taken time to think about it, I probably would have kept my mittens, because, after all, I did have a cart full of groceries and a few more stops to make. To this day, I can think back on that moment, and her deep and genuine gratitude, and I feel happy inside. I am able to re-visit the feeling of sheer joy that came from helping someone I didn't know at a time when I wasn't expected to. Those are the little things that make life grand!

Sometimes we can overthink a concept, idea or opportunity until the moment has passed. The ability to make decisions quickly can be the difference between getting something to market before everyone else, or after everyone else. It can be the difference between closing a sale or not. It can be the difference between being seen as a leader or remaining a follower. *Carpe Diem*. Be decisive. *NOW*.

Exercise: Decision Making

List a decision you've been wavering on, or an idea you've been hesitant to make a firm decision about. List the issue and then list three action steps you are going to take to begin to get the ball rolling.

BUSINESS ISSUE/IDEA:

ACTION STEPS:

LIFE ISSUE/IDEA:

ACTION STEPS:

Do it Now...Then Do it Again...

*The way to get started is to
stop talking and start doing.*

Walt Disney

The power of taking action is well touted in any book on success. However, I'd like to suggest that it's *consistent* action that is really going to produce results. You can get all fired up and work out six days in a row, but that's not going to produce long term results if you are not consistent. In fact, you're better off to work out twice a week for three weeks than to jam six workouts into one week, and then not head to the gym again for a month. Slow and steady wins over fast and sporadic every time.

In the early days of my business I sold bracelets online. I sold between five and ten bracelets a *month* for over eighteen months. But it was that steady presence in the market that led to being in the right place at the right time, having two very large clients find me, and allowing me to grow my business to where it is today. In business it's easy to implement something and then slowly let it slip away — social media, marketing, internal recognition, even writing thank-you notes or clearing off your desk at the end of the day. Make your goal not only to take action, but to take *consistent* action.

Exercise: Action Plan

List one action you would like to consistently make. Maybe it's exercising or taking vitamins or calling your top ten clients twice a year to check in. Whatever it is, list the action you want to practice consistently and then plan for it, right now, in your Google calendar, your planner, Outlook, or whatever method you use to keep your schedule.

CONSISTENT ACTION I CHOOSE TO TAKE IN MY BUSINESS:

FREQUENCY: (3 times a week, daily, etc.)

CONSISTENT ACTION I CHOOSE TO TAKE IN MY LIFE:

FREQUENCY: (3 times a week, daily, etc.)

☐ I HAVE WRITTEN DOWN OR RECORDED
WHEN I WILL TAKE THIS ACTION.

Monitor and Adjust

When it is obvious that the goals cannot be reached, don't adjust the goals, adjust the action steps.

Confucius

When we show up, not only do we need to pay attention to what matters, we need to monitor it if we want the maximum impact. When we monitor something we're taking it one step further than just paying attention to it. We're tracking our progress so we can make any adjustments needed to be certain we attain the results we're aiming for. That's why we have a scale in our bathroom. We want to monitor our weight and make adjustments to our eating and exercise to be certain we get the desired results.

There are lots of things in business that are critical to monitor: sales, inventory, personnel, expenses, marketing, and cash flow. If we want to play at the highest level, we have to monitor these factors in a systemized manner so we can make the necessary adjustments to obtain the maximum results — or to avoid a devastating crisis. Sometimes the only thing needed is a small, fine adjustment. Sometimes we need a complete overhaul! If it's currently February, and you know that in the month of August business will be slow and your cash flow will not be adequate to cover your expenditures, you can begin to make small adjustments now to compensate. We've all heard the old adage that 'the time to plant a crop is not when you're hungry.' Well, the time to discover you're $5,000 short for payroll isn't on the Friday afternoon when checks are issued. Monitor those things that really matter, make adjustments so you get to where you want to go, and divert any unnecessary crisis.

Exercise: Adjustments Needed

List one area of your life or business that you need to monitor that you currently are not. Then define the method you will use to monitor it. If you don't know how to monitor something, make a decision to find someone who does. (For less than $100 I had my accountant set up a Cashflow Analysis report. We've now used that same report format for over seven years!)

AREA TO MONITOR IN BUSINESS:

HOW I WILL MONITOR:

AREA TO MONITOR IN MY LIFE:

HOW I WILL MONITOR:

Eliminate Distractions

You will never reach your destination if you stop and throw stones at every dog that barks.

Winston Churchill

I believe one of the greatest hindrances to our fully showing up in life and in business is distraction. Between email, instant messaging, Facebook, cell phones, text messaging, Twitter, and a whole host of other distractions, it becomes challenging to show up and get anything accomplished. It is *impossible* to be consciously aware and distracted at the same time.

I was recently volunteering at my son's fifth grade field day and there was another mom assigned to the same activity. She spent more than half the afternoon on her phone: texting, checking Facebook, talking, or playing games. I really wasn't sure WHAT she was doing. What I was sure of was that she wasn't seeing the joy on the kids' faces when they managed to get a ring over the bowling pin, she wasn't relishing the sunshine and the chirp of the birds on that glorious spring day, and she wasn't connecting with the people surrounding her in that moment. She missed so much!

No matter how many days we have or events we attend, no hour is ever repeatable. So often, instead of *being present*, we distract ourselves with our gadgets. Put down the device and be present so you can show up!

Distractions are a major roadblock to productivity in our businesses too. It's easy to mindlessly sit down at our desks and check email first thing. We have our cell phone right beside us, and every ding, whir, or chime it makes takes us out of what we are doing. I recently read an article in which researchers studying brain waves explained how an interruption, even just a casual morning greeting, actually takes twenty minutes of our time. The study explained that even if the actual exchange is only a minute, it takes our brain approximately twenty minutes to get back to the place of concentration where we were prior to the interruption.

For centuries, actually millennia, our society has survived without being instantly available to everyone all the time. In my time management courses I teach "time chunking." It's a system where you plan a daily two-hour chunk of "focus time" without distractions. You will be amazed at the amount of work you can get done, not only *in* your business, but *on* your business if you block a few hours a day of total focus time without distractions. I have found it essential to balancing my life and seamlessly accomplishing the many things I do each day.

Exercise: Distraction-Free Zones

Here's my **business challenge** to you: For one week, do not check your email first thing in the morning. Come into your office and sit down for a minimum of two hours and accomplish something *before* you check email. If you have instant pop-ups letting you know there's a new email arriving, turn those off. To manually send/receive is to ensure that you're checking emails on your terms, not your computer's terms. And, unless the structure of your business makes it impossible (you have to be honest with yourself here), I want you to also turn off your phone for that two hours. Then record the results below:

Monday:

Tuesday:

Wednesday:

Thursday:

Friday:

Part One: Show Up

How did it feel to do something of merit before heading down the rabbit hole of email and phone calls? I have not found *one person* yet who does not instantly increase their productivity through this one tip.

Here's my **life challenge**. For at least two hours every night, turn off your phone and your computer and be completely present with your family. Then record the results below:

Monday:

Tuesday:

Wednesday:

Thursday:

Friday:

How did it feel to have uninterrupted time with your family?

What differences did you notice?

Look, Listen and Learn

Every man who observes
vigilantly and resolves steadfastly
grows unconsciously into genius.

Edward G. Bulwer-Lytton,
English politician and writer

Did you learn about "stop, drop and roll" as a kid at school during fire safety instruction? Well, if you're in the middle of a fire in your business or your life, you need to "look, listen and learn." To really show up in the most powerful way possible is to allow yourself to observe and listen.

First and foremost, it's about observing and listening to that quiet inner voice that gives each of us personal guidance and direction. Don't underestimate the power of listening to your own intuition. At the same time, we must listen to customers, clients, teammates, associates and supervisors. It's about listening and observing the people and situations around us to gain deeper insight and a perspective broader than our own.

I had been selling bracelets online for several months when I received a call from someone who had purchased one of my bracelets. This woman worked at the Jewish Community Center of Rochester, New York, and she requested a "fundraising packet."

My brain thought, "What the heck is a fundraising packet?" But my mouth said, "Well, certainly. I'll get one right out to you." As soon as I hung up the phone I Googled "jewelry fundraising." I didn't have a fundraising packet and fundraising was nowhere on my radar, but within forty-eight hours I had a fundraising packet on its way to Rochester. I was listening to what my customers were requesting, and being open to opportunities outside my current perspective.

I had never thought of allowing groups and organizations to sell my jewelry for fundraising. Today, ninety percent of my jewelry is sold through school, church and sports organization fundraisers. Once we're headed in a certain direction, the path will be revealed to us, if we'll just consistently show up, get out of our own way, and listen.

It's the same in life. It seems the less one has to say, the more one can learn. Try spending an evening with your family or a few friends, and say as little as possible. The elderly grandfather of a dear friend of mine always used to say, "If you listen to what everyone else has to say, you know what you already knew, plus what everyone else knows." Sound advice! It's astounding the insights you can gain simply by being quiet and listening.

Exercise: Listening Lesson

Today, when someone asks you a question, I want you to ask them a question back before answering. I want you to listen to their answer and observe things from their perspective. Then I want you to do it again. Make it a habit of not just answering a question, but asking more questions of them and seeing if you can foster a new perspective or discover a new opportunity available to you. Do it both in your business and in your personal life.

IN BUSINESS:
Question Asked of Me:

My Response:

What I discovered that I might have missed had I not really listened:

Part One: Show Up

IN LIFE:

Question Asked of Me:

My Response:

What I discovered that I might have missed had I not really listened:

Yes, Yes, and Yes

Never allow a person to
tell you "no" who doesn't have
the power to say "yes."

Eleanor Roosevelt

The whole package of showing up is not only to be present, but to be open to give once you're there. Our company motto is: Find a way to say "yes." It is one of the greatest advantages of small business over big business, which often has multiple layers of approval that even the simplest change must pass through.

My first response is always "yes." You want special packaging for your upcoming event? *Yes, we can do that.* You want to take that set of jewelry and sell it as two separate pieces? *Yes, we can do that.*

You want a different chain on that standard necklace? *Yes, we can do that.* In small business, there's no reason to say "no!"

The great thing about saying "yes" is that you can always change your mind later and say "no." I've found the following triangle can help get you out of most circumstances if you've said yes and you don't think you can deliver.

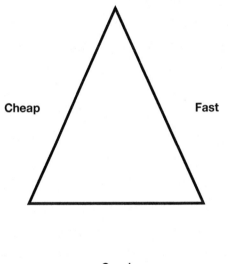

The diagram above shows three options for any situation: cheap, fast, and good. I explain to clients that I can say "yes" to two of the three. They can have it cheap and fast, but it's not going to be good.

They can have it cheap and good, but it isn't going to be fast. Or they can have it good and fast, but it's not going to be cheap. It always brings a smile — and a realization.

This works for both product and service industries. I've used it successfully with both my product (jewelry) and my services (coaching and speaking). I've found it to be true in hundreds of businesses in all industries, from restaurants to construction, from medical care to consulting. So it doesn't matter what question I'm asked, the answer is always "yes." Then I show them their options. Your business will grow faster and your life will become more exciting if you find ways to say "yes!"

In life, when we start to say "yes," things just seem to flow easier, especially as a parent. When I intentionally observed my answers, I found many times I was automatically saying "no" to my kids when I could actually say "yes." Why couldn't the kids empty the linen closet and use all those sheets to make a cool fort? Why not jump on the trampoline in the rain? Will it really hurt to have a popsicle before dinner just this one time? It feels good to say "yes." It has the effect of making life feel like more of an adventure. Try it today. Every time you find yourself ready to say "no," re-evaluate. Is there a way to say "yes?"

Exercise: The Experience of "Yes"

Sit where you are right now and repeat "yes" out loud a few times and feel that vibration. Then say "no" and feel that vibration. Record your observations below.

When I said "Yes" I felt:

When I said "No" I felt:

This really isn't that complicated. You can *feel* the difference between "yes" and "no" just by saying them out loud. Can you imagine the change in your business, and your life, when you change your predominant vibration to that of "yes!"

Get GRAND with Your Goals

Start doing what is necessary,
then do what is possible, and suddenly
you are doing the impossible.

St. Francis of Assisi

Whether you're a fan of goal setting or not, it doesn't matter, because goal setting works. In fact, if you're going to make all this effort to show up, I think you might as well be pretty clear on what you're going to accomplish while you're here. And I'm not talking about small, puny, easily achievable goals. I'm talking about big, grandiose, outrageous goals.

There's evidence to support that big goals are actually easier to achieve than small goals. The reason: you've got more momentum. More drive. More motivation to make them happen. You're simply more passionate about them!

Part One: Show Up

There's a story of a wealthy philanthropist who was asked to raise ten million dollars to build a new wing on a hospital. He set his goal and within six months he had raised the ten million dollars. His church, learning of his tremendous success, asked him to be in charge of raising $10,000 to renovate the church kitchen. He readily agreed figuring it would be easy compared to the goal he had just achieved. However, he quickly found that he couldn't do it. He wasn't excited about it. It wasn't a goal that made a real difference in his life or in the world. Adding a wing to the hospital — he knew the type of impact that would have in the world. But the church kitchen? He finally just wrote the check himself.

Each year, on the first day of January, I write twenty-seven goals: three goals in nine different areas of my life. The nine areas are:

1. Family and friends
2. Spirituality
3. Business and career
4. Wealth and finances
5. Health and body
6. Play and fun
7. Love and romance
8. Personal fulfillment
9. Artistic and creative

These categories have evolved over the years. I used to only do the first five categories. Then about ten years ago I decided I just wasn't having enough fun and I needed more play in my life. So I put an emphasis on play that year, and I've never looked back. I added personal fulfillment for those goals that just didn't fit in anywhere else. Artistic came from the need to create and enhance the beauty and movement in my life. Love and romance was added to be sure I'm giving my most precious relationship the attention it deserves.

Perhaps you've heard of SMART goals (specific, measurable, attainable, realistic and trackable). I decided I wanted a different kind of goal, so I make my goals GRAND goals.

G = guaranteed

R = recorded

A = authentic

N = noble

D = daring

That's the quick reference guide. Here's a more detailed discussion.

G = *Guaranteed* goals! Your goals are pre-ordained to happen just in the asking. The only reason you won't achieve a goal is because either you decide you no longer want it or something better comes along.

R = Your goals must be *recorded*. There is power in writing something down, so they must be written down.

A = They must be *authentic* to you, meaning they've got to be something you want for yourself, not what someone else wants for you.

N = They must be *noble*, which means they help you or someone else and they're moral and ethical.

D = And GRAND goals must be *daring*. They've got to push you out of your comfort zone. Do not base them on your current reality.

I think the most important of all the letters is R, and that's because the most important thing is that you *record* your goals. You must write them down. For many years my goal was to be president and CEO of a million-dollar company. It wasn't SMART according to the acronym above, but it was GRAND! I wrote it down and repeated it daily, and most importantly, I believed in it! Above all else, physically write your goals down and then read them every day. I carry mine in the front of my daily planner. I'm still a pen and paper kind of girl. I like to see my schedule in black and white. I see my goals every time I open my planner — a minimum of five or six times a day. Put yours where you can't avoid them: the bathroom mirror, the front of the refrigerator, the dashboard of your car. Then take a few moments each day to look them over.

Exercise: GRAND Goal Setting

G = guaranteed

R = recorded

A = authentic

N = noble

D = daring

Take a few moments to write down what you'd like to create in your life. Don't over-think it! Below are the nine areas to get you started. You may not have goals in every category, or you may want to add categories I don't have listed.

1. Family and friends

2. Spirituality

3. Business and career

4. Wealth and finances

5. Health and body

6. Play and fun

7. Love and romance

8. Personal fulfillment

9. Artistic and creative

I encourage you to not leave this exercise here on this page. Refine your goals so you feel you've got the three most important goals in each category. Then write them or type them up on another piece of paper. Lastly, post them in places where you will see them, and read them daily.

"Show Me the Money" Baby

*Don't be afraid to take a big step
if one is indicated. You can't cross
a chasm in two small jumps.*

**David Lloyd George,
British Prime Minister from 1916 – 1922**

My husband, Robert, does not love business. He'll be the first to tell you so. He loves dentistry though and he's a fantastic dentist — one of the best on the planet, as far as I'm concerned. (And he's humble enough that he won't tell you that!) But he made one comment that changed the direction of my business forever.

It was in the early years of my business (for the first four years it was just me) and I had had a very busy day. On this particular day I had sorted beads, labeled bins and created a filing system for charms. That evening I was sharing with Robert how I'd been busy every day for months, but I still didn't have enough money to pay my bills.

Robert looked me square in the eye and said, "Well, why don't you do what makes you money then? Sorting beads doesn't make you any money."

How could I have missed that?

When we show up, we need to put our focus on the activities that will net the biggest dividend. If you're a life coach, then it's coaching a client face-to-face that brings in the cash. If you're a copier salesman, it's selling a copier, not memorizing a map of the city. If you're in plumbing, it's fixing a leak, not reorganizing your client list! I'm a firm believer that everything you do in your business matters: how you answer the phone, ship a package, or market your services. When it is what you *do* that matters, to get the most out of life and business, you must *do* what has the biggest payoff. In business, that's the activities that actually generate income. If you don't have enough money to pay the bills, quit re-organizing files or color coding your prospects and go make a sale!

It works the same way in life, too. Which is going to have the biggest payoff — an hour at the gym or an hour channel surfing on the couch? Is engaging with your children and enjoying time with them going to net bigger dividends than logging onto Facebook for an hour? Is listening to a personal development tape going to pay off more than listening to Pandora? In every moment that we show up, we get to choose how we spend our time. Do what will net the biggest dividend and help you reach your goals faster.

Exercise: My Top Three

List the top three *money making* activities in your business:

1.

2.

3.

Now I want you to take a Post-it note and write at the top, "Today I will focus on: _____," and then add the three activities you've listed above. Put that Post-it note on your computer and look at it every day. Begin to spend as much time as possible on those three activities.

List the top three *personal growth* activities that will make the biggest difference in your life:

1.

2.

3.

Now I want you to take a Post-it note and put at the top: "Today I will focus on: _____," and then list the three activities you've written above. Put that Post-it note in the drawer next to your toothbrush. (I'm making the assumption you brush your teeth at least morning and night!) Every day, begin to focus a portion of your day on each of those three activities.

Get Over It

The gem cannot be polished without friction, nor man perfected without trials.

Chinese Proverb

I understand that you probably would not expect to read 'get over it' as a strategy in a business book. But I think it's one of the most crucial things you must do if you're going to show up strong and play at the highest level in business and in life.

There isn't a person walking this planet that hasn't been injured, betrayed, disappointed, or lied to. Every single person you meet has a story. It's part of the human experience. Life happens — to all of us, personally and professionally. I've had companies knock off my designs. I've had clients declare bankruptcy to get out of paying debts and then open up for business again under another name. I've had employees log onto Facebook while on the clock.

The point? It's done. Get over it.

You can either spend your time harboring resentment and being angry about the ills you've suffered, or you can get over it and move on. You are going to be able to go much further in life and business if you choose to focus your attention on all the good things happening in your world. I don't have to work with unscrupulous clients. I can address the inappropriate use of time at work. I just can't hold onto these wrongs and become suspicious and jaded. The Bible says, "For whatever one sows, that will he also reap" (Galatians 6:7-8). We all reap what we sow and there's no benefit to holding on to an injustice that is over and done with. And remember, although we always reap *what* we sow, we don't always reap *where* we sow.

There are many people who have endured grievous hurts and deep sorrows in life. But I've met fifty-year-olds who are still sitting around blaming their rotten childhoods for their present circumstances. Come on! We all have pain in our past; every one of us. What separates those people who go on to create lasting happiness and outrageous success is that they forgive those who have hurt them, and more importantly they forgive themselves when necessary. When you refuse to forgive, the only person who remains hurt is you. It's time to get over it and move on.

Exercise: Getting Over It

For this exercise I want you to get a sheet of paper (or two or three depending upon how much have to get over!) Write down every person, situation, or circumstance you are still holding onto that you need to "get over." Then I want you to write a letter surrounding that situation, describing in great detail how you were affected and how it made you feel. Be brutally raw and honest. Remember, you are forgiving the person or letting go of the situation **for you**. Write until you have nothing left to write. Then take that paper and shred it, burn it or tear it in a thousand pieces. Emotionally release it as you physically destroy it. The goal is just to get it out of your body, on to paper, and left in your past – where it belongs!

11

Always Be Learning

He who knows most,
knows how little he knows.

Thomas Jefferson

Always be learning. Always. Always. Always. Learn. Learn. Learn. In business there is always more to learn. That's why most professional associations, from massage therapists to doctors to architects to teachers, have continuing education requirements. They want to make sure you keep learning. Aside from the technical skills required, it's important to keep learning about business and the new ways business is evolving. With the latest developments in technology, social media, online stores and e-commerce, there is so much to learn and keep up with. Fortunately, a lot of it can be learned online through webinars and tele-seminars. Allow yourself to be a student of business.

Without exception, the most successful people I've met are those who spend thousands — and even hundreds of thousands — annually on personal development. They are constantly investing in themselves to learn and grow. I have found that the people whom I meet at personal development seminars are some of the happiest, most enthusiastic, excited folks I know, and they're making the biggest difference in the world. When we improve and work on ourselves, we're also making the world a better place. Every positive thing you do to develop your own character has a ripple effect out into the world that allows your learning to help so many more people than just yourself. You might be learning something right now so you can be the vehicle to carry that knowledge to someone else who wouldn't receive it any other way. When you help yourself grow, you help the whole world grow.

Don't have money available to you (yet) to invest in books, audios, or seminars? Get yourself to your local library. Visit a used bookstore. I imagine that if you have this book in your hand, you're already focused on learning, and if you're like me, you could probably stay busy listening and reading from items that are already on your bookshelf that you just haven't gotten to yet! For a list of my personal favorites go to www.kimhodous.com/learn.

Exercise: Ten by Forty

I want you to look at your schedule right now and decide where you are going to fit in ten minutes of learning a day for forty days. This is not extra time you need to fit in somewhere; this is going to *replace* something you're already doing. Here are some options:

- If you listen to the radio in the car, just replace ten minutes of listening to the radio with ten minutes of an educational or personal development CD.

- If you get up in the morning and watch the morning news (or the evening news before you go to bed), just replace ten minutes of that with ten minutes of inspirational material.

- If you read the newspaper, take just ten minutes of that time to read something that's going to help you grow in your professional or personal life.

- If you sit in the lounge at lunch or on breaks, still do that; just take ten minutes of that time to fill up your mind with a book or CD that's helping you learn something new.

Now, commit to doing it! Fill in the sentence below and sign your name. Do it for forty days, and then just keep repeating for the rest of your life!

I, _____, commit

to expanding my mind for a mere ten

minutes a day for the next forty days. I

am going to do it _____

_____

_____.

I look forward to all the new things

I'm going to learn!

_____

Signature

_____

Date

Show Up. Be Bold. Play Big.

Part Two: Be Bold

To be bold is to stand out. It's an attitude. It's an approach to living life to the fullest so you can have what your heart desires. The dictionary defines being bold as, "standing out to be noticed, such as bold text or bold type." That's what being bold in business is about. It's about standing out from the crowd. It's about separating yourself from everyone else out there. In life, it's about standing up for the only you there will ever be.

There are so many ways to stand out. Being bold in business is nothing new. Henry Ford did it when he engineered the 'assembly line.' Sam Walton did it when he was the first business to put all the check out registers at the front of the store. Zappos has done it with their unparalleled customer service. In tough economic times, though, everyone plays it safe by following the lead dog and staying with the pack. I believe we need to take the exact opposite approach. Look at what everyone else is doing, and put a twist on it. Find a way to do it better or different.

Stand up, stand out and be **bold**!

Be Authentic

Be yourself. Everyone else is taken.

Oscar Wilde

The first and most critical thing you must do to stand out is really quite simple. You just have to be you. Sounds easy, doesn't it?

But stop and think: How can I be the best "me" to get noticed?

Here's how. Find your strengths and utilize them. If you're a nurturer, then be the one to bring a muffin to a co-worker who's going through a divorce, or be the one to make a fresh pot of coffee when it's down to the last cup. If you're an encourager, offer to walk during lunch with a teammate who's trying to lose weight or stop smoking. If you're an organizer, then help set up the best systems your office has ever seen. Take your strengths and use them to become the very best you that you can be.

If you're a business owner, identifying your strengths can also be a good barometer for hiring your staff. The most important thing to look for when hiring new personnel is someone to complement your strengths and fill in for those things you don't enjoy or you're no good at. Ironically enough, they usually coincide. As you grow your team, amplify your strengths and compensate for your weaknesses.

Having an authentic business is critical too. I'm a straight shooter and I'm going to call things as I see them. As a success coach, I'm not going to hold your hand and let you wallow in what happened to you in the past. We'll look at it, get the lesson from it, get over it, and move on. This style works for some and not for others.

It's important to be very clear about your company approach in marketing materials; you want to attract the right type of client so everyone experiences success. Howard Schultz, founder and CEO of Starbucks, said, "Mass advertising can help build brands, but authenticity is what makes them last. If people believe they share values with a company, they will stay loyal to the brand." Authenticity will bring you relationships, connections and experiences that will create lasting success! To be genuinely happy and successful, you must first be genuinely you.

Exercise: Authenticity

IN BUSINESS: Where in your business do you feel like you're compromising who you are?

What can you do to be more authentic?

IN LIFE: Where in your life do you feel like you're compromising who you are?

What can you do to be more authentic?

Be Different

*The hardest struggle of all is
to be something different from
what the average man is.*

Charles Schwab,
American steel magnate

When I started selling jewelry in fundraising, I had to find a way to stand out and be different. What was it about me that would make people remember and choose my company? A-ha! My jewelry was all custom-designed by me. All the other jewelry being sold in fundraising at that time was being bought off a factory showroom floor in China. In an industry where product is driven almost solely by price, no one ever dreamed that a "designer" product was possible. I had been designing my jewelry at my kitchen table for years, but soon I realized this was what made me stand out from the crowd. It gave me the advantage because I could tailor my designs to what I knew would sell in the fundraising market.

To be different and live boldly in life you have to quit worrying about what others think. Most people are so self-absorbed that they really aren't focused on you anyway! Too many people have gotten caught up in "keeping up with the Joneses," wearing clothes with just the right label, living in the right neighborhood, and driving a certain car. Psychologically, children go through a documented phase from about fourteen to twenty-one where their peers become more important to them than their parents. Okay, we can give them a break. But I've met forty-five-year-olds who are still trying to fit in!

Figure out what makes you stand out and capitalize on those advantages. Instead of trying to fit yourself into everyone else's definition of what's cool, find out what's cool about you and then share that with the world! A great place to identify your personal character strengths is to visit www.authentichappiness.org and take the VIA Survey of Character Strengths. It takes about forty-five minutes and will give you some awesome insight into what your personal strengths are. Be bold. Be different.

Exercise: Being Different

List three unique things about yourself that you like:

List three more:

Now, list ways you can capitalize on those differences and use them to enhance your life, your business, and the lives of others.

Be Fearless

*Avoiding danger is no safer in the
long run than outright exposure.
The fearful are caught
as often as the bold.*

Helen Keller

At a very early age, we are programmed to be afraid. Our parents were well meaning, but the messages we received were often born of fear: be careful, don't talk to strangers, lock your doors. I understand they were meant to keep us safe. I've said the same things as a parent, but the reality is that they're all messages of fear. As the mother of five, I can promise you the times I've said "be careful" far outweighs the number of times I've said, "Hey, be daring today." It's the same in business. Sometimes we're so busy being careful that we miss the opportunity right in front of us.

The amazing part? We really have *no idea* what's going to happen in the future. In the early 1950s a group of the nation's best scientists made a time capsule of predictions for what would occur in the 1960s. When they opened it in 1970, they had missed it all. They missed computers, walking on the Moon, and medical advances. By projecting into the future, they couldn't figure out what would be available to help us solve problems, heal people, or transfer knowledge. If the greatest minds of the times can't figure it out, why do we think we can? Why fear that what we need in the future won't be available to us?

The problem with fear is that it's paralyzing. One summer I was in the hot tub with a bunch of other moms. The kids were playing in the baby pool nearby. One of the toddlers teetered over to the big pool and promptly fell in. The mom of the toddler stood up — and froze. Quick as a flash one of the other moms jumped out of the hot tub and had the toddler out of the pool before she even knew what hit her. It was interesting to observe the mom's reaction. She was rendered helpless to do anything. Her fear had paralyzed her.

Being fearless in business is crucial to your success and your growth. When we get fearful, we become paralyzed and we lose all innovation, momentum and excitement. I had feared Twitter for years, so I finally went online, set up an account and tweeted! No big deal! What was I so afraid of?

The antidote to fear is movement. Even if you're scared, you've got to jump anyway! If you experience fear, take some action. Do something. It's in the taking of action that we cause the fear to go away.

Exercise: Jump Anyway

Where in your business do you need to "jump anyway"?

Where are you letting the message of "be careful"
hold you back instead of keep you safe?

What actions can you begin to take to move through
some of these fears?

Where in life do you need to "jump anyway?"

Where are you letting the message of "be careful"

hold you back instead of keep you safe?

What actions can you begin to take to move through

some of these fears?

Be Optimistic

*The last of the human freedoms
— to choose one's attitude in any
given set of circumstances,
to choose one's own way.*

**Viktor Frankl,
Austrian neurologist and psychiatrist**

I'm fascinated by a study that was done at the National Science Foundation where they discovered that 95% of what people think is negative and that 90% of what you think about one day is carried over to the next day. So it's critical that every day we are vigilant in keeping our thoughts positive, because the bulk of what we think today is going to carry over into tomorrow. If you really want to be bold and stand out, focus on the good in everything and everyone who comes into your sphere of influence.

Part Two: Be Bold

A 1995 article in the *Journal of Personality and Social Psychology* found that Olympic athletes who win bronze medals are actually happier than those that win silver medals. The silver medalists tended to focus on the negative. They focused on the idea that if they'd done a little better, they might have won gold. The bronze medalists tended to look at the bright side. They focused on the idea that if they'd done a little worse, they wouldn't have won a medal at all! Our success and happiness truly depend upon where we focus — the positive side of things or the negative.

One reason we need to focus on the good and strive to bring out the best in every situation is that imagined disasters often never come to fruition. Mark Twain said, "I am an old man and have had many troubles in my life, most of which never happened." Have you ever noticed that most of the things you worry about never occur? I have gone to great lengths imagining how I am going to interact with a customer. I play the conversation out in my head with every possible response they might throw my way. And then when I finally talk to the customer, the conversation goes in a totally different direction. Instead of focusing on the details of the conversation, I find it far more effective to simply focus on the desired outcome of the conversation. This holds true for employees and co-workers, and even children and spouses.

Exercise: Focus on the Positive Outcome

Is there any area of your business you tend to worry about?

What is the desired outcome in that area?

What steps can you take to focus on the outcome of that situation versus the details of it?

Is there any area of your life you tend to worry about?

What is the desired outcome in that area?

What steps can you take to focus on the outcome of that situation versus the details of it?

Be Non-Judgmental

Judge not lest ye be judged.

Matthew 7:1

We usually think of this Biblical command only in life, not in business. We learn to practice it as kids in Sunday school. We don't often think about being non-judgmental in business. But let me tell you, you will definitely be bold if you dare to carry this over into your business.

It's important not to judge your clients and customers. I dated a man in college who worked at a car dealership. He loved to tell the story of the day a kid rode in on his bicycle. He had on blue jeans and a hooded sweatshirt. There were three salesmen on the floor that day, and two of them laughed and gladly let the new guy, Scott, have this dubious prospect. Scott treated him no differently than he would have an adult in a business suit or a doctor in scrubs.

They test drove three or four cars. Scott got him the specs on each vehicle he wanted to see. At the end of the day, the kid pulled a wad of hundreds out of the pocket of his hoodie and paid cash for a brand new car. He threw his bike in the trunk and took off. You can imagine Scott's grin as his co-workers gawked!

When you pre-judge what your clients can or cannot afford you are putting limits on the growth of your business. Don't think for your clients. You never know their circumstances. When billionaire Sam Walton, the founder of Wal-Mart, was alive, he drove a 1979 Ford F-150 pick-up truck around town. If you didn't know who he was, you would think he couldn't afford the gas to go in it!

It's the same with a new product line or idea. If you've thought of it, then there's merit in it. You need to test your idea, but don't pre-judge it as good or bad until you've systematically tried it out.

It's the same with the people you meet. If a person is here on this planet, then they have merit. We are all valuable and are here for a reason. It may not always be evident to us now, or even in this lifetime, but every person has a purpose.

Exercise: Judge Not

Are there places in your business you're pre-judging, selling clients short, or shooting yourself in the foot by making up your mind about something before you've given it a chance? Explain.

Is there someone in your life that you're pre-judging before you really know them? An employee? A client? A friend or family member? Explain.

Is there a product line you want to look into but have decided it won't work? Is there research that could be done to see if it has merit? Explain.

Be Aware of the Lesson

*One day in retrospect the years
of struggle will strike you as
the most beautiful.*

Sigmund Freud

I once read the story of Corrie Ten Boom and her younger sister Betsie, who were in a concentration camp in Nazi Germany. They had been separated from the rest of their family, but they were determined to survive. The younger one, being more naive, decided that to survive they would have to stay positive and optimistic. The older sister agreed to try. As the war came towards its end, and the Allies got closer, the treatment in the camps became worse. Many of the young women were beaten, tortured and abused. Yet the younger sister insisted that they stay positive, and find some way to be thankful for what they had. Time went on and although it seemed as if things couldn't get any worse, they did. Their dormitory became

74

absolutely crawling and infested with fleas. Betsie decided that they had to be grateful even for the fleas. Corrie replied, "The fleas! Betsie there's no way even God can make me grateful for a flea." Betsie quoted from the Bible, "Give thanks in all circumstances. It doesn't say, 'in pleasant circumstances.' Fleas are a part of this place." So they stood between the rows of bunks in that horrid place and gave thanks for fleas.

I don't know if you ever thought about being thankful for fleas, but I don't think most of us, in the best of conditions, could find the fortitude to be thankful for fleas. But that was the attitude of these young girls. It was only in the very last days of the war that they discovered that the Nazi supervisors and guards would not enter their dorm because they were terrified of disease…and the fleas. Even fleas, at times, can be a blessing. There's a lesson in every experience if we just look for it.

When you have an experience, positive or negative, be aware of the lesson that is there for you to learn and grow from — regardless of whether the lesson reveals itself immediately or not.

Years ago we had our clients place purchase orders in March for products to be delivered in July and subsequently sold in the fall. One season when we went to deliver, we had a client change his mind and refuse his product. We were left with thousands of units of jewelry and no place to sell it. We learned our lesson and began gathering a 30% deposit at the time an order was placed, and it's never happened again! Be aware of the lesson that is there to learn. When you look at life's experiences as a way to learn and grow, rather than being a victim to them, you'll definitely be living more boldly than most. Our culture teaches us to lay blame and make excuses. Being bold is about abandoning blame and excuses, taking responsibility, learning the lesson, and moving on.

Exercise: Learning Lessons

Think back over the past month to one positive experience you had in business. What was the lesson for you to learn and take forward?

Think back over the past month to one negative experience you had in business. What was the lesson for you to learn and take forward?

Think back over the past month to one positive experience you had in life. What was the lesson for you to learn and take forward?

Think back over the past month to one negative experience you had in life. What was the lesson for you to learn and take forward?

18

Be in Right Relationship

Always do right. This will gratify some
people, and astonish the rest.

Mark Twain

Being in 'right relationship' is about being in integrity and doing the right thing. Early in my business career I had a mentor who helped me grow my business by 700% in one year. Dan was crucial in helping me gain admittance into a prestigious trade show and in helping me design my programs and my brochures. Without him, I wouldn't be where I am today. Or at least I wouldn't have gotten here as quickly.

After that first year, when Dan was basically no longer helping me, I chose to be in 'right relationship' with him. In the previous year, Dan had spent countless hours helping me, purely out of the kindness of his heart. I actually asked Dan at one point if he wanted to go into partnership with me. He declined. He said he was trying to 'phase out, not gear up!' My sales had soared. I was making money. My business was thriving. Dan and I had no contract. He never asked me for a dime. Ever. Yet, at the end of that first year, I decided to give Dan a percentage of my sales. I felt he deserved it. He hadn't worked for me, but he'd generously shared his expertise. So I just put a check in the mail to him with a letter explaining that I was not only going to give him a percentage of sales for this past year, but that I was going to give him a percentage of sales for the next year as well.

Dan was blown away. He didn't expect a penny. At this point I probably only spoke to Dan once or twice a month. Because I had jumped into the industry so deeply and I now knew people he didn't, sometimes he called to ask *me* a question. I was introducing him to potential clients and suppliers! He was ecstatic and felt I more than compensated him for the help he'd given me. I believe the goodwill and good karma I created from doing the right thing propelled my company further than it could have gone without that message to the universe of, "Reward me. I'll do the right thing when I succeed."

Being in 'right relationship' isn't just about when things are going well, either. I've made so many mistakes in business that I could fill up a book twice this size. That's just part of the process. What I've learned is that if you screw something up, you have to always make it right. One year, I tried a new factory and their delivery was NOT as promised. Their delay meant I delivered my clients' orders late. This had never happened before. I made sure that every client received a personal phone call to explain the situation and to apologize for the inconvenience. It was important to me to stay in 'right relationship' – even when I was the one who was wrong. The best way to make things right is through communication. It's amazing what a simple phone call can do. There's basically no cost to this, but the net return is huge.

Exercise: Making Relationships Right

Where in your *business* is there a little (or big) mess you need to clean up? It might be with a former customer or supplier. It might be with a present or former employee. If there's any situation you think back on that makes you feel uncomfortable, that's the one. Take the necessary, and possibly uncomfortable, steps to put that situation in 'right relationship.'

Where in your *life* is there a little (or big) mess you need to clean up? It might be with a former boyfriend/girlfriend. It might be with a family member, friend or neighbor. If there's anyone you think it would be uncomfortable to run into at the store, they're the one! Take the necessary, and possibly uncomfortable, steps to put that situation in 'right relationship.'

Be Excessive

Make happy those who are near, *and those who are far will come.*

Chinese proverb

There are not a lot of businesses out there falling over themselves to 'over deliver.' Providing excessive value will guarantee you and your company a **bold** reputation and help you to stand out. There are so many ways you can do this, and most of them won't even cost you much money.

We have a regional franchise of sub shops in the area where I live. When you walk through the front door, you're greeted by someone calling out from behind the counter, "Hello! Welcome!" Unexpected. Easy. Free. We had one supplier that included a Jolly Rancher candy in every order they shipped to us. I can't imagine Jolly Ranchers cost much more than a penny each, but it always delighted us — and still does.

Part Two: Be Bold

After attending my first fundraising association tradeshow, I noticed that the biggest issue facing our industry was the number of students participating in their school or church fundraiser. Over the years it had dropped from 70% participation to as low as 30%. After the show, the association sent us a directory of names and email addresses of every attendee. I entered all those email addresses in my database and sent out a survey. I asked each member to share their 'best practices' for boosting participation. I promised everyone who submitted an idea a copy of the final report.

From the survey I found out that members had done things like getting the principal to kiss a pig, giving every child who sold one item a special gift, offering a hot air balloon ride to kids who sold more than ten items, and awarding cash prizes. The list was amazing. The final result was over 200 ideas on how to increase participation, contributed by almost 100 different member companies.

Not only did it restore my faith in the industry — after all, sharing your best ideas with everyone else in the industry is pretty generous — but it also put me on the map as a supplier who was concerned about distributors and wanted to help. My efforts didn't go unnoticed. Seven years later I still have people mention that report and tell me that to this day they look through it as they're setting up their prize programs and rewards for fundraisers.

Show Up. Be Bold. Play Big.

In life it's equally as easy to over-deliver. One of my favorite lines in the movie *Pretty Woman* comes when Julia Roberts is hiding something behind her back. Richard Gere, having assumed it was drugs but discovering it was only dental floss, says, "You surprised me. That doesn't happen very often." She responds, "Well, you're lucky. Most people surprise the hell out of me." More often, we're surprised in a negative way. Be bold and surprise people by exceeding their expectations. You will stand out from any crowd, and, as a bonus, your success and happiness will skyrocket!

Exercise: Expectations Exceeded

What are some small things you can do in your business right now to over deliver? How can you surprise and delight your clients?

What are some small things you can do for the people closest to you right now that will surprise them in a positive way?

Be Risky

The dangers of life are infinite, and among them is safety.

Goethe

Making decisions or taking actions that are risky is necessary for living a bold life or developing a bold business. Be risky, but not reckless. Being risky is about taking calculated and intentional chances, and not always playing it safe.

I remember applying for my first teaching job. It was in a small town in central Arizona where my husband of two weeks was opening his first dental practice. I applied at the local high school but they had no openings, with none on the horizon. This school had a teacher turnover rate of zero; once someone got a job there, they stayed. I knew if I was ever going to be employed in this town, I was going to have to be bold. However, they did need substitute teachers. So

I began subbing. Then I had an opportunity to teach for a full week when a teacher was going to be out for surgery.

I got permission from that teacher to take the content she wanted me to cover and come up with my own lesson plans. I then went to the principal and explained I would be teaching in my own style all week, and I invited him to come into my room at any time during that week to watch me teach for an hour. I told him if he saw me teach he'd be so impressed, he'd find a way to hire me!

He came in and observed my teaching — and he soon found a way to hire me! He said he'd had teachers on staff for twenty years who had never invited him into their classroom. It was a risk. But I was confident in my ability and I was prepared. When we take a risk, we can remove many of the risk factors simply by being prepared and doing our homework.

It would have been reckless if I hadn't known my material, prepared lesson plans, learned the kids' names, or had decided to just let the students watch movies all week. Being reckless is throwing caution to the wind without proper planning. I had planned and was ready. It was a calculated and intentional risk. Be risky, not reckless.

Exercise: Being Risky

Where in your business are you playing it too safe? Where are you holding things too tightly? What can you do to put your business out there in a bigger and bolder way without being reckless?

Where in your life are you playing it too safe? Where are you holding yourself back? What can you do to put yourself out there in a bigger and bolder way without being reckless?

Be Open

*It's wonderful to have
a beginner's mind.*

Steve Jobs

In 2001, I attended my first trade show in the fundraising industry. I was excited, and frankly, a little nervous about attending. I'd never been to a trade show. They don't have trade shows for school teachers; at least, twenty-five years ago when I was a teacher they didn't.

The first evening of the trade show there was a welcome reception. The association provided free food and drinks, so I knew attendance would be heavy. Even though I was exhausted and all I really wanted to do was order room service, I put on my best smile and headed to the reception.

Once there I worked the room, introducing myself and meeting as many people as possible. This is an industry where most people have known each other for years and relationships run long and deep. I found myself on the outskirts of many groups, but I'd look for someone else who wasn't engaged in a conversation and I'd introduce myself.

As the reception was coming to a close, I saw two men, both a little older than I, with kind faces and quick smiles. They were in blue jeans and sported a laid back demeanor. They looked like they'd just arrived. They weren't talking to anyone else so I made my way over. "Hi. I'm Kim Hodous, the owner of Rockwood Jewelry. This is my first year here and I don't really know many people. Who are you guys with?"

They answered, but I didn't recognize their company; I was so new I wasn't familiar with most companies. They were warm and welcoming, and most importantly, conversational. In fact, when the reception ended, they invited me to join them for dinner. My soul still craved the solitude of my room, but I decided that since I was there, I better be open to what came my way. So I said yes.

During dinner, we bonded. We didn't just talk business; we talked kids and family, hopes and dreams, wins and losses, politics and religion. We left no stone unturned. There was tons of laughter, and before the night was over, we had each even gotten a little misty eyed over the touching stories we'd shared. This was a night of connection. I loved these guys and I'd just met them! As the evening came to a close, I made them promise to come by my booth in the morning.

The next morning when they showed up at my booth, I was stunned and speechless. My name badge had one ribbon on it, signifying me as a new member. Both these gentlemen had ribbons down to their belts. They were charter members of the organization. They served on various committees. They were Ambassadors for the Board of Directors! Oh my. With whom had I been to dinner? These were two of the biggest hitters in the industry and I'd been sharing my life's dreams, my fears and insecurities about being there…and my struggle with potty training my toddler!

But because I was open, their company was the first to take a chance on me, and they placed an order that very day. In the following year I parlayed their order, and the confidence it created within the industry, into more than $626,000 in sales!

See what happens when we're open and simply allow ourselves to be in the flow of life? When we release resistance and are open to new energy, more can flow through us and to us. I repeat often and emphatically, "I lead a charmed life. I am always in the right place at the right time, meeting the right people." Be open. Be bold.

Exercise: The Experience of Being Open

Think of a time you were open and things flowed easily: doors opened, you met the right people, you were able to help others, and you felt good. Write down what you were doing and how you felt.

Think of a time you were closed off and things did not flow easily: decisions didn't produce the results you wanted, and the people and resources you needed to make something happen were not available. Write down what you were doing and how you felt.

Now, which one would you rather experience? Make a choice to be in the flow, and repeat often and emphatically, "I am always in the right place at the right time, meeting the right people." And if you'd like, add in "I lead a charmed life." It's a great life to lead!

Be Still

*Silence is a source of
great strength.*

Lao Tzu

Being still might sound like it contradicts everything else I've written thus far, but it doesn't. Being still complements the other strategies I've shared. Taking the necessary actions to show up, be bold, and play big allows us to stand out, be a leader and become a role model in our area of service. However, we must balance the activity and movement with stillness, quiet, and silence.

I read an article years ago that discussed how everything in life is the polar opposite of something else. The concept is that your high can't go higher than your low goes low. This is a very good thing for those of us who had challenging childhoods or deep sorrow, because our joy and success can now go as high as we previously went low! In other words, the bigger your failures, the greater your successes;

the deeper your pain, the grander your joy; the more intense your disappointment, the more profound your fulfillment. It is the same philosophy which Newton's Third Law of Motion advocates — that for every action there is an equal and opposite reaction.

As you begin to show up, be bold, and play big, your life is going to be moving faster and there are going to be more people and opportunities around you. To temper all that movement and activity, you also need stillness. It will bring you a calm, centered groundedness that is integral to change and growth.

Volumes of scientific research are available to validate the health and psychological benefits of stillness. Just taking a few minutes at the beginning or the end of your day to be still, reflect, and go within can make measurable improvements in chronic pain, anxiety, high blood pressure, serum cholesterol levels, substance abuse, and blood cortisol levels. All this just by being still! Imagine how your life and your business will improve when you counter the movement and activity with quiet and stillness.

Exercise: Being Still

I want you to set your phone for a one-minute alarm. Then for one minute I want you to just sit and breathe and keep repeating to yourself, "Be here now." Don't let any other thoughts come in, just "Be here now." Let your breathing become rhythmic. How did you feel after that one minute?

Decide to take five minutes at some point each day and simply breathe and repeat to yourself, "Be here now." Commit to it. Consistently. And watch the magic reveal itself to you.

Show Up. Be Bold. Play Big.

Part Three: Play Big

Playing big is about cultivating an expanded mindset. Plain and simple — it's about how you think. To go somewhere you've never gone, or to accomplish something that's bigger than you are, you've got to think a certain way and direct your thoughts towards certain outcomes. It's about mastering your mind and remembering that you're here for greatness. Playing big is about maximizing every bit of success, prosperity, opportunity and fun in your business — and your life.

Love What You Do

Believe in your business more than anyone does. Passion is at the top of the list of the skills you need to excel.

Sam Walton

I have found that you cannot "*miserable*" your way to the top; you can only "*joy*" your way to success! Because if you miserable your way to the top, when you get there, you're still miserable! The people who are truly successful — financially and otherwise — truly love what they're doing.

There's a segment of our culture that has tried to convince us that the people at the top are unhappy — and it's just not true! In the old paradigm of limitation, there was a mindset that there wasn't enough room at the top for everyone. Those with that mindset thought if they could convince us that you have to step on people to get to the top, and you'll be miserable once you get there, then we'd quit striving to make it there! This is an outdated way of thinking.

To play big, you've got to love what you do or it's just not sustainable. The most successful people on this planet are the ones doing what they love. And I would venture to guess that if you know someone who's successful and they're miserable, they'd be miserable if they were poor and unsuccessful too.

It's essential that you absolutely *love* what you're doing and what you're selling, because if you're not excited about it, how can you expect someone else to get excited about it? A long time ago a jaded and cautious businessman told me, "Don't fall in love with your product." You know what I say? Bull! I say fall madly, deeply in love with your product. If we want people to reach into their pockets and take out their cash and give it to us for what we're selling, I think we better love it — a lot!

When we do the things we love — whether that's playing a round of golf or practicing yoga, taking an order or making a sales call — when we're happy, we make those around us happy. When we're doing something we love, we shine, and we make our family and our friends happy; we make ourselves and our employees happy; and most importantly, we make our clients and our customers happy. Love what you do.

Exercise: Loving It

Make a list of all the things you love about your business, your product, and your clients. Don't stop until you reach 100!

Make a list of all the things you love about your life, your family, yourself. Don't stop until you reach 100!

Now focus on these things and add to the list as more come to you.

Dream Big

Who wants a dream that's near-fetched?

Howard Schultz,
Chairman of Starbucks

I love the story of the man who sat by the river fishing. Every time he caught a fish, he held it up against a stick, and if it was longer than the stick, he threw it back in the river. A young boy watching him wondered why he kept throwing the big ones back, and so he asked the fisherman why he was doing that. The fisherman replied, "The stick is the size of my frying pan."

So often we do that with our dreams. We dream small. We play it safe. We pick a little dream that we know will fit in our frying pan, that will fit comfortably into this nice life we're living, and not push us too hard or set us up for failure. We decide if we go for that huge dream, we might get disappointed. We might get hurt. Someone might laugh at us! So we continue to play small, and therefore, remain small.

Show Up. Be Bold. Play Big.

From the day I decided to turn my hobby into a business, when someone would ask what I did, I would respond, "I'm president and CEO of a million dollar company." Their eyes would widen and they'd look enormously impressed. I would offer no explanation. I *was* president and CEO of a million dollar company; it just hadn't fully materialized yet. And that was my standard answer when my sales were only $4,000 annually. You can't expect to *begin* where you want to end up, but you must *know* where you want to end up. To play big you must dream big!

Your business will never rise higher than the vision you have for it, and neither will your life. You can't end up with a million dollar business if your dream is to just be able to pay the bills. Your dream may be to simply supplement your income from a full time job. Maybe it's to impact thousands of lives or change the nature of commerce in the world. Whatever it is for you, define it, and then DREAM IT!

Exercise: Dreaming Big

Close your eyes and begin to breathe deeply. From this place of relaxation, think back to what your dreams were when you were young. Go back as far as you can remember. Record those here:

Then breathe deeply again, and think back to when you first started your business or career. What were your dreams for your business/ career at the beginning, when you started? Record those here:

Now going back to the place you started, and integrating that with where you are now, define what BIG is for you in THIS MOMENT. What would make a BIG difference in your life right now?

Act As If

*Act as if you were already
happy and that will tend to
make you happy.*

Dale Carnegie

Our dog Porsche weighs a whopping six pounds, yet I've seen her back a 100-pound black lab down our driveway. She has no idea how small she is! She acts as if she's an alpha dog – and so that's how she gets treated.

From the very outset of my business I had a vision of where I wanted to go. I wanted a large office with a high tech phone system. I wanted to be president of a million dollar company. I wanted to work with a group of highly supportive motivated women.

I created that. But even in the beginning when I had none of that, I acted as if I did.

I remember buying a $100 phone "system" from Sam's Club. It had one main phone and two extensions. There were three mailboxes — one for each extension. I had this message on my answering machine: "For Kim, press one; for shipping, press two; for billing, press three." I made up three separate messages for each one. They didn't need to know I answered all three mailboxes and all the extensions sat on the corner of my own desk. Now I actually do have all those departments, and a few more. In the beginning, though, I was just acting as if I did.

Similarly, if you want to weigh thirty pounds less than you do now, act as if you already do. Do what people who weigh thirty pounds less do. They go to the gym, they eat healthy; so, you do the same thing. Whatever it is you would like to create more of in your life, act is if you're already there and make your decisions from that place. Act as if, and so you will be!

Exercise: Acting As If

Think of an area in your business where you don't feel you've represented yourself well. Maybe it's your business cards, the sign in front of your office, your answering machine message, or maybe it's your letterhead. List things below you can begin to do to "act as if" you are where you want to be.

Think of an area of your life where you've not represented yourself well. Maybe it's keeping your purse messy or your car trashed. Maybe it's your appearance or your self-discipline. List things below you can begin to do to "act as if" you are where you want to be.

See It for Yourself

*What we see depends mainly
on what we look for.*

John Lubbock,
Pioneer of evolutionary theory

Equally as important as acting AS IF you are where you want to be is SEEING yourself there. It's going to be easier to play big if you already see yourself there. Visualizing something is on a subtler level than acting as if, but it's just as critical. It accesses a different part of your brain and engages all your senses including touch, taste, smell, sight, and sound. Visualization has proven to work because our subconscious mind can't tell the difference between something that's real and something that's imagined. That's why we cry at movies. We *know* the movie scene isn't real and yet we still *believe* the experience we see unfolding before us.

When we can experience something in our minds' eye before it actually occurs, we have a greater chance of experiencing it in our physical reality. Visualization has long been a part of the training ritual for Olympic athletes. Often called 'mental rehearsal,' athletes are trained to see their perfect performance, over and over again, in their mind. They are taught to use repetition through visualization to enhance their skill, in the same way they use repetition during physical practice. Begin to see yourself as successful and happy, living a rewarding and satisfying life, over and over again, and you'll soon be there.

We will only see what it is we're looking for. I went to see the movie *Seabiscuit* with a dear friend of mine. She has no children. She is an animal lover and has trained both horses and dogs professionally. When we came out of the movie and began discussing it, it was as though we had been to see two different movies. She, as an animal lover, had totally connected to the horse and the jockey's relationship to his beloved animal. As the mother of five, I connected to the boy's relationship with his parents and his heartbreak at being separated from his father. To me, the story of Seabiscuit, the horse, was simply a vehicle to share the universal theme of parent-child relationships. To her, these relationships were merely side notes to the story about the horse and the deep connection between humans and animals. We both saw what we were looking for. That's why it's critical we 'see' and envision our success — regardless of where we currently are. Because whatever it is we're focused on, we'll find.

Almost every personal growth book, from the classics like *Think and Grow Rich* and *The Strangest Secret,* to modern day inspirations like *The Secret* and *Mind Powers,* extol the virtues of visualization. Seeing where you want to be will assist you in getting there even faster. It's critical we master our thoughts, but it's also critical we see ourselves and our businesses where we want them to be.

Exercise: Seeing It & Scripting It

I want you to close your eyes and breathe deeply for about one minute. Then I want you to, in your minds' eye, see your business, and your life, exactly how you'd like them to be twelve months from now. Bring in all five senses — see it, hear it, smell it, taste it, and feel it. See every little detail. Now "script" what you saw below. Write out in great detail the vision you have for your business and your life. (I personally do this every 90 days and it's amazing when I review the previous 90 days' writing. Often, a good portion of what I wrote actually happened!)

Celebrate All Successes and Failures!

If it's good, it's wonderful.
If it's bad, it's experience.

Eleanor Hibbert, British writer

Kids totally get the strategy of celebrating all successes – big or small. Kids can turn any ordinary moment into a reason to rejoice. Have you ever watched how children delight in a butterfly floating by? Their excitement in making a goal in soccer? Their laughter at a roly-poly? When did we as adults lose that? The Law of Attraction states that like attracts like. Kids get this concept, too — "I'm rubber and you're glue, bounces off me and sticks to you!" It's the idea that what we project, we become. When we embrace and celebrate all successes, whether our own or those around us, we draw more success into our lives.

In my company, we start every staff meeting with a "brag." We have everyone at the table give one success for the week. It sets a positive mindset for the meeting. We always celebrate birthdays by decorating the front door of the office so everyone entering the office is aware of the special day. We also recognize the personal accomplishments of members of our team. In the pursuit of obtaining my black belt in Tae Kwon Do, with every new belt I earn, I wear it to work and celebrate with the team.

It is equally important to champion the failures too. If you don't have any failures then you probably don't have much of a business. I have a list of failures that rivals my list of successes. So I celebrate those too. If you think back over your past, and you think about some of your most painful experiences, aren't those the ones where you learned the most? Those difficult times are the ones that help us grow, if we're open to the learning. They exist for our benefit, so why not celebrate them? Rather than looking at a situation as either good or bad, why not just see it as either comfortable or uncomfortable? It's usually the discomfort that produces the biggest a-ha's and fosters a deeper understanding.

When you let go of a victim mentality around failures, and just focus on the lesson learned, the mistake or failure can be viewed as a learning experience – and can be celebrated for the wisdom it brought.

Exercise: Let's Celebrate!

How in your *business* can you begin to celebrate successes? Where are there opportunities for acknowledging wins, accomplishments, and successes?

What mistake or failure do you need to let go of and begin to see the victory in it?

How in your *life* can you begin to celebrate successes? What wins, accomplishments and successes in your life can you begin to acknowledge?

What mistake or failure do you need to let go of and begin to see the victory in it?

Quit the Blame Game

People are always blaming their circumstances for what they are. I don't believe in circumstances. The people who get on in this world are the people who get up and look for the circumstances they want, and if they can't find them, make them.

George Bernard Shaw

If you're going to play big, there can be no complaining, blaming, justifying, defending, or excuse-making. The people who have made it to the top have done it because they've taken whatever life has handed them and worked with it. Tyrone "Muggsy" Bouges is a prime example. He is 5'3" tall and weighs 136 pounds. That is shorter than me by two inches and lighter than me by — well, let's just say that he weighs less than I do. Guess what he did? He was an NBA All-

Star. He played sixteen seasons of professional basketball and was paid over eighteen million dollars. He didn't decide that because he was only 5'3" he couldn't follow his passion and do what he wanted. He took what life had handed him, made no excuses, and made his career what he wanted it to be!

When you take 100% responsibility for your life, it means you're willing to work harder, study more, and practice longer than someone else. You don't make excuses for why you can't. You focus on the reasons why you can and you make it happen.

You can find hundreds, probably thousands, of people with far fewer resources, capital and knowledge than you who are continually playing big. Mattie Stepanek wrote countless poems and essays, delivered numerous speeches on hope and peace, and authored seven best-selling books, all by the age of fourteen, and while suffering from a rare and fatal neuromuscular disease that eventually took his life. It's taken me forty-eight years to finally share my message in these pages! What are you waiting to do? No more excuses! Those people who are out there playing in the biggest way possible are not making excuses or blaming others for what they haven't done. They're taking one-hundred-percent responsibility for where they are and what they're doing with their life, and they're making their dreams come true. Join me, and decide to be one of them!

Exercise: Taking Responsibility

Where in your business have you been making excuses, blaming (whether it's the economy, the government or the competition) or justifying your current position?

List three action steps (IE: Low sales numbers? Make ten extra calls...) you can take today to begin overcoming those excuses and justifications:

Where in your life have you been making excuses, blaming others or your past, or justifying your actions?

List three things (IE: Overweight? Walk fifteen minutes...) you can do today to begin overcoming those excuses and justifications:

Master Your Thoughts

*Be master of mind rather
than mastered by mind.*

Zen proverb

The morning after Barack Obama was elected the forty-fourth president of the United States of America, his campaign team was interviewed by **60 Minutes**. During the course of that interview David Plouffe, the campaign manager, was asked about their strategy for winning states like Indiana and North Carolina — states no one thought a Democrat could win. Mr. Plouffe responded, "First of all, we thought we could win." His response had nothing to do with what they "did," it had to do with how they thought. They believed they could win. His first response wasn't about their use of the Internet or social media or their legion of volunteers or the massive amounts of money they raised. It was about aligning their inner thoughts with their desired outcome. If it'll work for being elected president of the United States, it'll work in helping you build your business and improve your life!

Your outer world is simply a reflection of your inner world. If you do not master your thoughts around your business potential, your employees' productivity, your product quality, your customer service and your supplier partnerships — and those thoughts become negative, it will be reflected in what you experience. To get what you want in business and in life, you must first believe it, then live it from the inside out.

Often, when something is not the way we like it in our outer world, in business or relationships, we try to fix it externally instead of going within first. Have you ever had a day when nothing goes right? You wake up late. You can't find the right color socks. You spill your coffee. Your gas gauge is on E when you get into your car. You hit every red light. Your child forgot his lunchbox on the counter. And this is all before you even get to work....

I have found that the only common denominator on those days is that there's always something that's not right in my inner world. It doesn't have to do with any of those physical irritations showing up on the outside. I've dealt with all those discomforts and small frustrations before and they didn't throw me for a loop. It has to do with me! It has to do with my mental state and where my thoughts are focused.

Maybe I didn't sleep well. Maybe I ate too much sugar the day before. Maybe I was worried about something or my attitude was off.

Trying to fix things externally without going within is like trying to change the picture on the movie screen without changing the film in the projector. It's impossible. Unless we go to the source, the same thing is going to be projected on the screen.

Since our subconscious mind accepts everything at face value, it's critical that we monitor our thoughts with the diligence they merit. Nothing good comes from thoughts such as: *Business is a struggle. The government takes all my profit. Customers try to cheat me. You've got to step on people to get to the top. I can't be friends with my employees.* Because we attract what we feel, if we think and feel this way, it's what we'll experience. Now re-read these examples and notice how you feel.

When you surround your business with thoughts such as: *Business flows to me easily. I always make the right contacts. My customers refer other customers. My employees love and support this company.* This is what you'll attract. Re-read these examples and compare how you feel now to how you felt only moments ago.

Of course it takes more than that; you can't just sit around and think yourself into success. But your thoughts about your business and your success have a direct connection to your bottom line!

Exercise: Master Your Thoughts

Think about something you would like to create in your *business* (hire a new team member, set a sales record, redo the website, or earn an award). Write it in great detail, using all five senses, here:

Now come up with three simple statements that encapsulate this vision and align your thoughts with your vision. Take these three statements and connect with them once a day for the next forty days.

Think about something you would like to create in your *life* (a new partner, a new home, weight loss, or travel). Write it in great detail, using all five senses, here:

Now come up with three simple statements that encapsulate this vision and align your thoughts with your vision. Take these three statements and connect with them once a day for the next forty days.

Have Some Fun

Fun is good.

Dr. Seuss

There's a plaque that sits on my desk that reads, "If it's not fun, I'm not interested." Life is meant to be fun! I've never liked the idea of separating parts of your life into compartments like work, play, family, and spirituality. I believe they are all rolled up into one. I want Rockwood Jewelry to be where I live my spirituality — through interactions with my team, my customers, my suppliers and even the UPS man. I choose to integrate my spirituality into my work through doing the right thing, being kind, listening a bit more closely, and being a lot more patient.

Likewise, I don't want fun and play to be separate activities I do outside of work; I want work to be fun — and there are so many opportunities to have fun at work. I remember there was a woman I wanted to hire who worked in the food service industry. I knew for a fact that a portion of every day, she had to wear a hairnet. So when she showed up to interview, I had on a hairnet. She just cracked up. I explained to her that working at Rockwood Jewelry, she'd never have to wear a hairnet. She told me later she took the job because that interview was so much fun.

Every year before we prepare to go to our trade shows, we have a little role-playing session. We bring in popcorn and set up chairs like a theater and play out every imaginable question we may be asked on the trade show floor. We could do this sitting around the conference table, but it's so much more fun to play charades!

Another way to bring more fun into your work is to hire the stuff you hate to do. How much fun is it to do stuff you dislike? For me, that was shipping orders. Early in my business, I actually found myself almost hoping I didn't have any orders, because at that time not only did I have to process the order and make the jewelry, but then I had to ship it. I hated packing the boxes, printing the shipping labels — all of it. The first employee I ever hired was a college student and she worked only six hours a week. She came in for three hours on Tuesday and Friday mornings to ship orders. It cost me less than $50 a week and it made me so happy! As soon as I had that part taken care of, my fun factor went way up — and so did my sales.

I have found in life that grown-ups can just be way too serious. Especially parents! I have girlfriends who are a blast. But what I've noticed is that a group of fun-loving, laughing, crazy women can become totally serious and adult-like as soon as the 'children' arrive. All the fun, spontaneity and play go out the window! I've suggested in those moments that we show the kids our fun side, and it's amazing the way the kids light up — and then my friends do too. Think about jumping on the trampoline or playing dress up or just being a goofball with your kids. Make a funny face. Talk in a strange voice. Have some fun. They'll love it, and you will too!

Exercise: The Fun Factor

What are the three things you dislike doing the most at work?

What are some creative ways you can make those tasks more fun?

How can you delegate some of those tasks?

What are the three things you dislike doing the most at home?

What are some creative ways you can make those tasks more fun?

How can you delegate some of those tasks?

31

Allow Others to Help You

*Many hands and hearts
and minds generally contribute to
anyone's notable achievements.*

Walt Disney

Most people in this world derive personal joy and satisfaction from helping others. I think it's why volunteerism exists in our culture and programs like Big Brothers and Big Sisters have been going strong for over a century.

Remember my mentor, Dan? For a period of six months, I spoke to Dan almost daily. Dan made a huge impact in my life and in my business…because I let him. He would have helped dozens of other people had they let him. I responded to a handwritten letter Dan sent me. He sent out over twenty of those letters. I was the only person who replied to it. There are dozens of people out there who had the same opportunity I did — they just didn't let Dan help them. When someone offers information, insight, instruction, or advice, listen. You don't know who your next teacher will be or how they'll come packaged. Dan came in the package of a quirky, grandfatherly sage.

At one of my early tradeshows, someone was questioning me about my "margin" and I didn't know what it meant. That night at dinner I was speaking with a man and I asked about margins. He took a cocktail napkin and scribbled out the formula and explained margins top to bottom. I still have that cocktail napkin. He was more than happy to share what he knew. Most people are.

I can recount hundreds of stories where people I knew, or someone I'd never met before that moment, stepped forward to help. In life, it can be as simple as someone opening a door or getting something down from the top shelf you can't reach. I've met people who are suspicious of any kindness and feel there's a hidden motive. Not one of those people is truly successful and playing big in life or business. The art of allowing others to help us opens up the playing field and lets us experience success more quickly and easily than trying to do it alone.

I'm glad you were open to receiving what I wanted to share with you in this book because it makes me happy to give. I want to help you succeed. People all around you want to help you succeed, too. I've personally experienced this, and I bet you have also. You can choose to watch the news and listen to stories of people hurting people, but

I believe that is the exception, not the rule. When we allow others to help us, we give them the joy and satisfaction of sharing their knowledge and using it to help someone else. Allowing someone to help you also underscores your BIGNESS to them, because it demonstrates your openness to learn and grow.

Exercise: Allowing Even More

Below list a minimum of ten times in the past week someone has helped you. It can be as small as allowing you to go through the door before them. It can be as significant as introducing you to a potential client or giving you a testimonial.

For the next week, I want you to write "EVIDENCE" at the top of a page, and each night, record all the times someone helped you — big and small. Begin to focus on all the assistance you're given each day, and you'll find even more floods your way.

Give Back

*If America is the pursuit
of happiness, the best way to pursue
happiness is to help other people.*

**George Lucas, American film director,
producer and screenwriter**

The flip side to allowing others to help you is for you to help others. As much as you are assisted and helped every day, double your efforts to help others just as much. We have so many opportunities to give every day to our customers, our employees, our suppliers, our families, our communities, and even to strangers we'll never know. Giving back is a way of saying thank you for all we've been given.

Giving back doesn't need to consist of huge endeavors. If you have the time, resources and inclination to start a foundation, build an orphanage, or travel to other countries, that's wonderful. By all means give back in that huge and amazing way. As business owners and entrepreneurs, many of us are so busy running our businesses and lives that the task of doing something that large would be daunting. So I encourage you to give back in smaller ways, at least initially.

You can give back by offering your goods or services to someone deserving who cannot afford them. My husband does thousands of dollars of dentistry every year for families that need it but can't afford it. It may not be as remarkable as a mission trip where hundreds of children are helped, but I can promise it makes a huge difference in the lives of those families. All giving counts. You can give back by donating to worthy organizations. Each Christmas we donate thousands of pieces of jewelry to the Salvation Army, Toys for Tots, and Big Brothers Big Sisters. The jewelry is given as gifts or is used as stocking stuffers.

Giving back is acknowledging the bounty of what you've been given. It's saying, "Yes, I have enough to share." Since whatever we give away comes back to us in greater measure, the more we share, the more we have to share. Giving back honors all those people who helped you along the way. It's the concept of paying it forward. If we just keep the good deeds coming, everyone will be lifted up to a higher level and be playing an even bigger game.

Exercise: Giving Back

Just as you plan out your marketing for the year, I want you to plan out your giving for the year. Start with a quarterly basis, and eventually you might even want to plan it on a monthly basis. Below, record ways you can systematically give each quarter of the year.

January – March:

April – June:

July – September:

October – December:

Be Grateful for Everything, All the Time

Gratitude is not only the greatest of virtues, but the parent of all others.

Cicero

Gratitude is essential for playing big. When we are grateful for everything in our lives, we open ourselves up to receive even more. Daily gratitude has been a part of my 'creating period' (my quiet, centering time each morning) for many years. Creating a practice of expressing gratitude spills over into every part of your life. You begin to be grateful for not just the good, big, and most obvious things. But you begin to be grateful for the small, insignificant and even challenging things. A deep experience of gratitude makes all of life rich and rewarding. It allows us to step into the flow of life, and stop resisting what we're experiencing.

Part Three: Play Big

I was speaking to an entrepreneurial group of students at a large university; the class focus was selling licensed products to support the school. One student asked if they could sell on commission because the class did not want to purchase inventory outright. He said, "We've got a whole closet full of inventory. We call it our 'closet of mistakes.'" I said, "Every business has a closet of mistakes, whether it's physical inventory or ideas that didn't work. If you're in business and you don't have a closet full of mistakes, then you probably don't have much of a business."

There's no shame in having a 'closet of mistakes.' The power of that closet is finding the lesson you learned, adjusting accordingly so you don't repeat it, and then being grateful for it. You learned a lesson you probably would not have learned any other way. Think about an airline pilot. Would you want a pilot who had only flown in blue skies? I want a pilot who has flown in every kind of weather and survived to tell about it! Appreciate the gray skies, they have value too.

Resistance is one of the main road blocks to expansion. When we accept what comes our way, and then express gratitude for it, our world becomes limitless. I love the practice of the indigenous people in Africa who make a living through subsistence farming. Their challenge is that every few years, grasshoppers swarm their lands and eat their crops. When the grasshoppers come and eat their crops, the farmers simply eat the grasshoppers. They don't resist and complain. They are just grateful for what they have, which in that moment, is grasshoppers.

It's noble to be grateful for the good things that come our way, but if we want to play at the highest level, we must also be grateful for the challenges. Be grateful for everything, all the time.

Exercise: Eating Grasshoppers

Think about a recent failure in your business. Something that didn't turn out the way you wanted. What can you be grateful for in that experience? What good came out of it?

Think about a recent disappointment in your life. Something that didn't turn out the way you wanted. What can you be grateful for in that experience? What good came out of it?

Conclusion

It doesn't matter where you start.
What matters is where you're going.

Kim Hodous

I was recently leaving a large convention center after giving a keynote speech, having shared my journey from being a stay-at-home mom and novice entrepreneur to becoming a successful business owner. After speaking, I had shaken hands and heard the stories of many of the people in the audience — always one of my favorite things about speaking. Just as I was about to exit the large glass doors of the convention hall, a woman came hurrying down the corridor calling my name. I stopped, looking forward to hearing another story. That wasn't her mission.

She took both my hands in hers, looked me deep in the eyes, and asked one question: "What did you have to do on the inside to make the jump from $20,000 in sales to over $600,000 in sales in one year? Not the business tactics, but what things did you have to change inside you?" It was a good question. One I couldn't answer very well on that day. One I hope I've answered through the writing of this book.

These thirty-three strategies are the things I did to make that jump. It's my deepest wish that they make the jump a little easier for you.

I want to assure you that wherever you are right now on the journey to show up, be bold and play big, you are right where you are supposed to be. Also know that as you begin to show up, be bold and play big, you can transform your life, and your business, into one glorious adventure. I know first hand. I've done it. I hope you will too. There are very few of us who dare to accept full responsibility for the ride we're on — happily embracing all the twists and turns, the ups and downs — and then doing whatever it takes to charge full steam ahead along that glorious path, or abruptly change directions if needed.

In sharing these strategies, I've given you the blueprint to increase your success and your happiness. When you take the time to show up and DO the things that make a difference – set goals, say yes, take consistent action, pay attention — you're showing up with a different vibration, a different frequency, and you'll attract new energies, people and experiences into your life. You'll reach a new level of success. Embrace it. **You deserve it.**

When you live boldly, you're BEING the most authentic YOU possible. Your attitude will improve. Your outlook on life will shift. You'll embrace each experience with a new awareness and understanding that everything that happens *to* you, happens *for* you and your biggest job is just to BE. Be aware. Be open. **Be you. There's no one better to be!**

Playing big is the most fun of all. That's what PLAY is — it's FUN! Playing big is throwing off the shackles of reason and daring to live the grandest, most fun life imaginable. Grabbing ahold of the vision that you're BIG and you matter. Celebrating all life's pains and pleasures and trusting that what, and whomever, comes your way is coming to help you play at a higher level! Playing big is about giving voice to your dreams and trusting that if you want to make it happen, **the world is ready — and waiting — for you!**

As you begin to integrate the strategies I've shared, changes may not happen instantly, but they can happen easily. Just allow yourself to be open to showing up, being bold and playing big in a whole new way – and watch tiny miracles begin to unfold. Celebrate each one. Trust yourself. It doesn't matter where you start. What matters is where you're going. **Now get going!**

If you enjoyed, *Show Up, Be Bold, Play Big*, Kim Hodous is the Ideal Professional Speaker for Your Next Event!

THE KITCHEN TABLE CEO™

KIMHODOUS

Kim Hodous is a sought after speaker who will leave your audience inspired, entertained and informed! Her high energy and fun presentations will not only delight, but will deliver a message that's dynamic and impactful! Kim uses the power of storytelling to ignite audiences to make positive change so they are more empowered, motivated and successful.

Kim believes everyone can SHOW UP, BE BOLD and PLAY BIG — regardless of age, gender, background, childhood, or current situation. Everyone has the power to live the grandest life possible. Let Kim show your audience how! Kim's most requested topics include:

- Inspiration and Motivation
- Leadership
- Time Management
- Goal Setting
- Communication

She also has special programs for 'women only' audiences. If you would like to know more about booking Kim for a keynote, breakout or workshop, please contact her office at 888-784-7489. Or email questions to me@kimhodous.com.

Share this Book!

Quantity discounts are available. Please contact us for a quote. We also have personalized, autographed copies available.

CPSIA information can be obtained
at www.ICGtesting.com
Printed in the USA
LVOW04s1153100916

503986LV00003B/3/P